A HUMAN MOON

Copyright © Alleliah Nuguid 2023

All rights reserved. Including the right of reproduction in whole or in part in any form.

This book is published by **DYNAMO VERLAG**

Capitol Hill, D.C., Echo Park, Los Angeles, Seattle, and St. Louis

Cover design by Derek Cornett

Printed in the U.S.A.

10 9 8 7 6 5 4 3 2 1 blast off.

DYNAMOVERLAG.com

PRAISE FOR ALLELIAH NUGUID AND *A HUMAN MOON*

Alleliah Nuguid's *A Human Moon* deals with culture and cultures intimately and abundantly, with fiery imagination, intellectual daring and rich verbal music.
–Robert Pinsky, author of "At the Foundling Hospital"

The poems in Alleliah Nuguid's terrific collection, *A Human Moon*, give us a look at the future of American poetry. They reach into both Filipino and American storytelling and cultural practices, considering where story sits beside or bleeds into myth. Along the way, they comment (often wryly) on horrors pop-cultural, ecological, and elemental; on jealousy or the failures of romance and parenthood; on genetic legacy; on navigating multiple identities; on gender; on our animal selves. Expressing themselves often through sharp wit, through camp, and through bumps in the night, they remain always brainy, always lyrical, and always and ever inventive and engaging.
–Katherine Coles, University of Utah, author of *Wayward* and *Look Both Ways*

Whether considering *Jersey Shore* or a 19th century anthropological study, Alleliah Nuguid's poems are electric and estranging, unsettling any conventional demarcations between the natural and human, real and surreal, the grotesque and the beautiful. In *A Human Moon*, ancient myths weave indistinguishably into our contemporary world while figurative concepts become literal identities: a young woman ghosted by a lover might, for example, be an actual ghost herself, while the horror movie trope of a cabin in the woods becomes an actual part of the reader's body, the cabin itself not just "a plot on the map" but a structure "inscribed on your own back." In this wonderful, weird, and always surprising debut, we find a fascinating blend of autobiography and fable, ecocriticism and race theory, where any body might finally become a "reproducible ornament": a brilliance, a monster.

–Paisley Rekdal, Poet Laureate of Utah and author of *The Night My Mother Met Bruce Lee: Observations on Not Fitting In* and *Intimate*

I really enjoy the voice and urgency of these poems. A little Kathryn Nuernberger, a little Pimone Triplett. From the first page on I am hooked. From a craft perspective, I like how this author writes a line–all the breaks feel intentional, smart and well-timed. I also really enjoy the subtle humor that is threaded throughout these poems. I'll even forgive the haibun with "haibun" in the title… As a transfemme, I think I'm legally required to love the barbie poem. This one's a winner for me.

–Rivka Clifton, Poetry Editor for Dynamo Verlag

Nuguid's construction of lines strike an excellent balance between the odd and sonically surprising and the measured and fluidly unfurled. I was constantly delighted by the language and our slow immersion and blending into nature and folklore. The poet experiments with form nailing couplets, scattered free-verse, as well as compact packets of image and sound, making the book feel like a whole cluster of variegated leaves belonging to a larger, unified, naturalistic and identity-driven concept.

–Lucian Mattison, author of *Reaper's Milonga*, *Peregrine Nation*, and *Curare*, and Poetry & Translation Ed. for Dynamo Verlag

In her debut poetry collection *A Human Moon*, Alleliah Nuguid combines verbal resourcefulness and acoustic play with an appropriately-global command of folklore and mythology—Philippine and Greco-Roman—to depict a realm of constant and sometimes violent metamorphosis. Cosmogony, theogony, catastrophe: these are the ancient words that describe the blurt and flare, not only of worlds in formation, but of the human self in formation, in her work. Sometimes the most interesting poetic companions are both formidable *and* vulnerable: Nuguid is capable of being both.

–Karl Kirchwey is the author of *Stumbling Blocks: Roman Poems* and six other books of poetry, and Professor of English and Creative Writing at Boston University

The startling poems in *A Human Moon* use lyricism to disconcert. They explore and strip away layers and surfaces, engaging a vast range of material, from horror films to Filipino folktales, exposing social and political as well as personal trauma and portraying the monstrous as uniquely human. Alleliah Nuguid's description of the bat who "watched/from her perch/alone, inverted" might almost be an ars poetica. Her eye is as unfailing—"in California (lollipop palms/lolling their dull heads windward) "—as her language is unflinching: "I was a rose and my thorns/ grew inward." This highly original collection will fulfill the mandate of its final line: "Endure, endure, however impure."

–Jacqueline Osherow, author of *My Lookalike at the Krishna Temple* and *Dead Men's Praise* and Distinguished Professor of English at the University of Utah

In Alleliah Nuguid's *A Human Moon,* a dangerous and endangered natural world ("amphitheater of chaos") serves as a backdrop for more internal landscapes—questions of ancestry and identity, the arc of romantic passion and attrition. Nuguid's knife-edged voice repeatedly summons images of inversion and reflection, of things being not as they seem—a Philippine myth in which the stars are the "shattered child" of the estranged moon and sun; a meditation on Narcissus in which his "wrinkled image" is "an effigy in water intended/to shatter." Collectively the poems produce the exhilarating feeling of being always on some brink. A stirring, thrilling debut.

–Maggie Dietz, author of *That Kind of Happy* and *Perennial Fall* and Visiting Professor of Creative Writing at U. of Boston

A HUMAN MOON
Alleliah Nuguid

*for my ancestors
whose names I do
and do not know*

CONTENTS

Excarnation	1

/

Meditation with Tymbals	5
Poem Ending With a Line From Jersey Shore	6
Variations on Received Wisdom	8
Neither/Nor	9
"Interesting Results of Professor Woodworth's Anthropological Studies"	11
Self Study	13
After Sappho and Catullus	14
Feed	15
World Made of Sugar	17
Flamingo-Eyed	19
The Seams	20
Theories	21
Aubade With Sand	23
The Earth is a Man	24
Manananggal	25
Pangaea	26
Crossing the Bay Bridge	27
Environmental Empathy	29
Environmental Empathy	30

//

The Mirrored Room	33
First Divorce	35
At the Mall	37
Haibun in the Event of an Earthquake	38
Accomplice	40
Ars Poetica	41

Why the Filipino's Nose is Flat	42
Plane Poem	43
Ghosting Monologue	44
Tale of Two	47
Everyday Exorcism	48
Postscript	49
Murder Cabin	50
Poem	54
Dinner Party	55

///

Lost Art	59
Hibiscus Depths	60
Fable For Your Hands Only	61
Circling	62
Barbie's Dream Home Invasion	63
Objects in the Mirror Are Closer Than They Appear	64
The Window and the Mirror	66
Mukbang Diptych	67
O Rubber Glove	69
Palinode	70
Melancholia	71
X	73
Spirit Canoe	76
Bardo Again	77
Animal at the Watering Hole	78
Prodigal Daughter	79

*

Kantian Love Story	83
Notes	84
Acknowledgments	85

EXCARNATION

In the vulture's domain, I am native
to death. Every backward step home
I bore my body, which clutched in turn
the season's fashion. Now it is time
to serve myself

                        up as hors d'oeuvre
on a plateau platter, garnished with carnage.
I've eaten, Lords. No, I have gorged
on provisions of unknown provenance,
I've gourmandized without asking how or why
or whom I fed

                        upon, nor have I
considered the vulture and what must pass
through her gullet for her to pass judgment.
My form holds light as fingers laced, and waits.
She pecks politely at my flesh, slightly
masking her distaste at

                        what she finds, what I
no longer hide. Bald head rouged with blood,
she emerges with a verdict, surges skyward,
abandoning my bones to calcine in the sun.
Bird of paradise, bird of prey: she will bear me
back again one day,

                        swathed in pearly linen,
                        partially forgiven.

MEDITATION WITH TYMBALS

Here, sound drowns sound.
Cicada song funnels into

tympanic collision, tactile
echo rounding the cochlear

spiral. Message swollen
as dew and as contained,

compounding like the rain.
The transformed Tithonus

petitions for death, or else
that other myth of love: un-

failing call and response…
—The voice and the voice

are beside the point. The sun
grazes the window and sheds

a husk of heat. Somewhere a scissors
runs its tongue across its teeth.

POEM ENDING WITH A LINE
FROM *JERSEY SHORE*

Where Narcissus goes, so does
his doubled thirst.

At the shore's brink, the wrinkled image—

Where he leans, *he* leans
into the collusive collision.

An effigy in water intended
to shatter.

     / /

"Don't you understand
that the body itself

is illusion,"
       he says to his mirage,

"and without it,
we can be cancelled."

     / /

That germ of the desire to tear oneself
from mirrors—

What part of "don't you understand"

don't you understand?

VARIATIONS ON RECEIVED WISDOM

        She can't have her cake and also eat. She can't
buy the baker's yield and still feel the cool of the nickel in her
palm.
        Nor sit in this chair and sit in the other, too.
    She hears the neighbors' voices from downstairs: either
they're fighting or they're making love—forgiveness
        genuine or pretended. She
can't sit in the pews at Mass and also ascend
to the belfry and pull the rope for all to hear,
        including Him. While there, or there, she must
want God or want the taste of the Medjool dates. The wolf's
hunger, sated by the lamb's life.
        She can't eat her cake and eat her cake. Nor
    take a knife to divvy the sugary thing; nor refuse.
It must be enough to have
        or else. The full barrel, the drunk wife: Choose.

NEITHER/NOR

He that is neither one thing nor another has no friends. —Aesop

Birds and Beasts rose
to the question of double
dominion: land and sky
a single kingdom, ruled
by the victor of war. The Bat
watched from her perch.

Angling their snouts at
the Bat, the Beasts
entreated her to ally with them.
She hid hirsute breast behind
her papery wings:

I am not
a Beast I
am a Bird

See this desire for flight
fulfilled; this taste for sweetness,
ache only fruit can sate

Later the Birds, bound
for the battlefield, paused
to recruit the Bat. She shielded
wings behind her furred body:

*I am not a
Bird I am
a Beast*

*See these ears open
to echo; this mouth
to appetite for
wildness, for meat*

At the final moment,
Birds and Beasts reached
an agreement and bisected the earth
per natural divisions. The Birds
swam across sky; the Beasts

dangled from the grass; the Bat,
spurned by both, watched
from her perch,
alone, inverted.

"INTERESTING RESULTS OF PROFESSOR WOODWORTH'S ANTHROPOLOGICAL STUDIES"

The most interesting of these lessons are the least
easily obtained / They are those whose subjects are hidden
in the jungles of Central Africa / in the barren islands of
our own Pacific possessions / in the cold and cheerless wilds

At the Louisiana Purchase Exhibition / never before in the lives
of living / anthropologists had so varied a collection / of
primitive races been brought / together fresh / wild / savage /
placed at the disposal of scientific / observers / under
conditions so helpful to research / The comparative

anthropometry of these unique little / brothers and sisters of
ours / cannot fail to interest / The little fellow's / head would
come about / to a level with the second / button on the
American's coat / his tiny legs / yet undeveloped by civilization
/ Tests were undertaken to determine

the validity of the theory that as / certain races / less civilized
than / our own have keener eyesight / than ours it is to be
inferred that / civilization has injured our sight / Quite / on the
contrary / the least civilized races examined / Negritos /
Ainoos / pygmies /

had the poorest sight / Although able to recognize more distant objects than the American / the Filipino is far less keen than he in distinguishing / colors / Their inferior color sense was not attached / to any particular color / but was universal

SELF STUDY

I was a lily pad laid flat
under rain. The pond absorbed
the shock; I absorbed the pond.
Each drop tremored across me.

I was a comb and I only knew
hair—coral incandescence
within the dark shimmer.
Coded narrative of teeth.

I was a rose, and my thorns
grew inward.

I was a coat rack arrayed
with the garments of outsiders,
my arms angled in orison.

Rings radiated
from heartwood
when I was a tree
and terminated
in burnt-orange
ornaments,
embers falling.

AFTER SAPPHO AND CATULLUS

He seems the mark of Priapus, your own
Personal dupe of the gods, reproducing
Your ogle—he leans in nearer to hear
        That nymphean voice—

It taunts my ill-made heart to tantrum,
Seeing you with your equal. Senses
Disarray: the flaccid tongue flops,
        While your intercourse

Cancels everything else in my wasted
Earshot. Eyes flash a chosen dark.
Underarms soak, fragrant…
        The undercurrent

In my skin: flame, impotent flame.
O welaway! it appears I am short
Of dying. Though greener than grass
        And more idle.

Impoverished of death.

FEED

radiant screen
reconfigures for free

>*you were nowhere*
>*now   you are here*

you are ablaze
in a blue
wash of light
imitation
of firmament

decant your
crafted self
lift it to
the influenzal azure

>*sodiment*
>*withheld*
>*in glass*

syncopated voices
from a fever dream
the curated feeds
the preternatural
pitch of each post
striking pewter

the fabricated
echo takes form
as firm as thought

you and I,
we have an old-
fashioned
connection
string hinged
tin-can telephone
hum kinetic
ocean
chant sirenic
updates

WORLD MADE OF SUGAR

Another tree whose name
I will never know towers

over powdered cars, its brittle tendrils

terminal, unreachable,
fragile as dendrites

or spun sugar. When I exhale

breath and smoke
become inextricable. If winter is

expected, inevitable,

why do I feel unnumbered
penumbras surround us? My American

Spirit whittles to the nub—

    *

In California (lollipop palms
lolling their dull heads

windward) you told me

you were dying. You were
not wrong, exactly, though

untimely. I found myself

a time zone away
from your hospital bed,

making your fist with my hand.

FLAMINGO-EYED

Like the flamingo, I   am a social   creature. Colony-

                bound and one leg folded into a nest of pink.

The other,   mud-stirrer   of saltwater   prey. (Unlike

the flamingo: salt, water, and pray.)   And my body, too,

is reproducible   ornament.   How the shallows

wash over the ankle, brittle-   seeming as a spider's.

How the plumage pigments with carotenes. How the coloration

      inspired the myth of the firebird which builds its own pyre

of frankincense,   cassia, myrrh,   strolling

through death as through a revolving door. This life, a hotel liaison.

Next, it will rise   from a suburban   lawn, companion

to worms and gnomes. None   too base for this terrain.

None too untrained, anchored   in dirt and the lingo of forebears.

THE SEAMS
after "Heart of the Matter" by Otis Kaye

I have it here I have
a heart and it is paper
-ed green : green the color
of the whole of the hole :
an oval of laurel : tender
: legal : an unblinking eye on the ob
-verse : or is it reverse : maybe
perverse : of that heart suspended
by string : here it is the heart of
what's the matter : what's the matter
of the matter : seventy-five
per cent cotton : the remainder
linen : it does not grow on trees
: in wombs : the accumulating
one : one : a buck : a bone : a stack
of bones : the heart thus
tendered : & lovingly rendered : green
how much I want to have
green : I almost have it : it nearly seems

THEORIES

Before the beginning there was nothing. All was confusion and then

*

void shot through with light. Two figures took shape and name: Tungkung Langit, Alunsina. Between them, an immense heat.

*

Ten billion degrees Fahrenheit.

*

They lived at the summit of heaven where the air was always warm. He set to work imposing order, envisioning lines. As for her, she spent the days combing her hair by the water.

*

Fibers of time threaded into sequence.

*

In a fit of suspicion, she sent the sea breeze to spy on him. When he learned this, he was doubly incensed: not only was he not unfaithful, but there existed no one else to be unfaithful with! Alunsina, banished, vanished back into the void.

*

All matter subjected to fusion or decay.

*

And then the celestial body barren of her. Distended space around it.

*

He carved out the sky but it spoke not with her voice
He fashioned the sea but it knew not her face
He howled at the moon he had yet to make

*

Glistening divisions; thunder, even now, approximates a name.

*

Subatomic particles cooled into jewels in the afterglow.
Remember: in the beginning there was

*

not only not but no one.

AUBADE WITH SAND

Orange sea mottled with dimples. Faraway slopes, skin smooth
as a grape.

                        In this biome, only us & the other
     diurnal creatures, desolate together. Your eyes

                                  a forest jade: vernal

sculptures crystallize. Difficult not
to see the plains as a pulsing heart, though difficult, too, to
look. You say: *You don't*

          have to say it. I say anyway: *I didn't know I wanted*
this and now

                                           I have it.

Through our hands as through the waist
of an hourglass, sand slips & joins again

                              the ocean of itself,

coalescing in ecstatic

     echo: it curves into treble clefs, reclines into operatic
beacon: our desert aria resounds.

THE EARTH IS A MAN

Who else could handle this
        craftsmanship? From Earth's perfect
physique sprung Nature, tender
        baby back, under Heaven
the Hall of Men. Orion
        hitches his star-belt of kings.
The Sun, brilliant alembic
        rendering image into
clarity, is the dangling
        ball too bright for mortal sight.
Gaze, instead, at the Moon, cast-
        away of the Earth's spare parts,
soundless siren, fingering
        her rabbit foot necklace as
she draws your dinghy to doom.
        Only Dawn can save you now.
Blink of synthetic lashes.
        Rose-blush, expertly applied.
She whispers the men awake:
        Now's the time for you to rise.

MANANANGGAL

My eye is the vessel for your image,
but inverted: like a bat from a limb,

legs clinging to the corneal brim.
So I gaze groundward, mask the edge

of my voice with meekness. Woman
by day, I demur, mouth hymns,

I am agreeable as a lamb.
The curtain falls at eventide, when

I am absolved of this body, this sin—
Split at the hips, I set my legs aside,

still standing in skirt and sandal, then slide
wings out from beneath my skin.

I roam over tin roofs in search of your unborn.
Tik-tik, tik-tik: the music of a woman shorn.

PANGAEA

Giants turn in slumber under a comforter of water
and earth, terrain reforming beneath the sky's
wolf-whistle and glint of tooth. The isolate masses
crawl to the meeting place with halting slowness—
reluctant lovers—and then fit together
like pieces of a face-down jigsaw, navigating contours
by touch. The seas, too, merge into a single azure
ornament. Yet the dissolution is equally destined.
Pangaea will tear itself into plurals. Go the way of the pager.
Our seats are already saved in this amphitheater of chaos.

CROSSING THE BAY BRIDGE

What curative was that,
driving there, driving back,

attempting to suppress
through repetition?

In a car full of voice
dictating fiction, or songs

that weren't for me.
The sky was a lagoon

that could torrent any moment.
The bridge a set of stilts

upon a quake.
What was it I was

in the strenuous task
of forgetting? The photo

in its envelope still,
in one of the boxes

I had yet to move.
Attempting to suppress

through repetition
was one solution,

where the tenor of
a voice overlaid mine,

and the black of the bay
alloyed with the sky.

ENVIRONMENTAL EMPATHY

Inside me, a woman
is turning into
an aspen. Her organs
flatten into an order
of rings. Her eyes
grey and multiply
along her silent
vertical. When I
breathe, I rustle
her leaves.

ENVIRONMENTAL EMPATHY

Inside me, too,
is a man. He
boasts of his
closeness with
the aspen woman,
gesturing at the
heart he carved
into her trunk.
He claims they
are meant to be.
If she still had
her mouth, he says,
she'd agree.

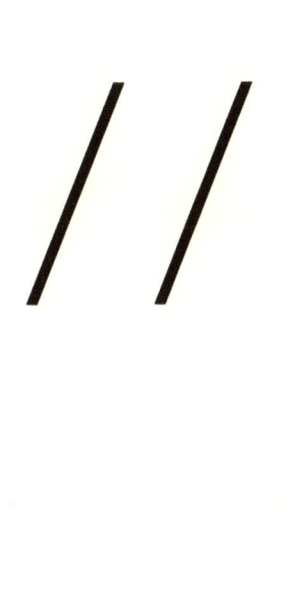

THE MIRRORED ROOM

1.

In accordance with the law
of reflection, light
striking a surface recoils in a fixed
trajectory. The angle of
incidence is equal
to the angle of reflection just as the mirror
image equals
the image that is being mirrored.

What counts as
incident. What counts.
Who says.

2.

An infinity mirror amounts to instantaneous
mitosis. Placed in its sight, you proliferate

in infinite triplicate, multiplying
and dividing into a piecemeal feast of self.

You grow smaller; you grow farther.

As you shrink away, distance gorges
on the expanse you leave behind.
That interval
of carrion. Capacity

a zero-sum game.

3.

A table spoon. A carving knife. A lake,
acid, salt, or otherwise. A car's new
coat. A window at night. The sunflowers
in your lover's eyes. Nature unnaturally
remade into mirror.

Whelmed, I cannot look.
Or: I can not look.

FIRST DIVORCE
After a Philippine myth (Manobo)

All light was concentrated in the union of wife
and husband: moon and sun. Where they went, light
followed. When they left, darkness took.
Day and night permeable as primordial earth.

It was the moon who cradled their child
in ferns and rocked him to sleep. The sun's own
love was danger: he could not hold
his child without burning him.

Once, with the moon gone, the sun peered
at the sleeping boy. Larynx slammed with love.

> *Echoing admonitions — from*
> *The beginning, impossible*
> *To listen —*

He unanchored himself.
He scooped up his child
and kissed that forbidden face.

> *Without pain — Without*
> *Waking — In an instant*
> *Incinerated*

When the moon returned, the charred boy
was still hot and dotted with errant flame.

The moon lifted her boy's body
and smashed it against the sky.
Shards dispersed into stars.

In return, the sun imbued the taro leaves
with his heat and hurled them at her face.
They clung: permanent scars.

Repentant, the sun pursues
the moon each day, illuminating
revolution. The moon matches
her husband's speed, maintains distance,
carrying the remnants of their son.

To this day, they have not spoken.
Each century, they halt their motion
and face each other in silence—
the sun sweating flares of remorse,
the moon staring blotted with shadow,
the shattered child brilliant, irradiating.
World looks on in darkness.

AT THE MALL

a piercing machine
aimed by a teen at the small of the still

healing lobe

barely misses, punctures air instead.
I take my best friend's safety-

pinned wrist

and pull her into the crush of bodies, body
sprays, sprays of forget-me-nots. She

cartwheels into

the current with the gymnast grace which will later
fail her once and never again but for now

initiates us

into the food court where our
boyfriend is waiting, saving our seats. He asks me to

marry him

and I decline. He asks and asks, caching delicious
refusal. We spend all Sunday this way.

HAIBUN IN THE EVENT OF AN EARTHQUAKE

We're driving the Bay Bridge, three years and counting. Twenty-sided dice slung around the rearview click and knock. My hand on the wheel. Your hand on my hand on the wheel. Radio tuned to white noise. You change the station. Now the car swells with your voice, telling the story:

*

The city roads were paved with blinking eyes. We marched to our place on the hill, rising over row houses alight with midburst stars. Jacaranda waving in our wake. Mist made lacunae in the sidewalk's grey. Then the slope steepened: an unhinged equation. The slick cement lodged in our fingertips, and rain ran us down.

*

Remember the morning you found me calcified? Voice had hardened overnight and sunk into my thorax. You brewed tea with ginger from the garden and massaged loam into the skin around my navel. The carapace yielded; I collapsed into you like a child. That day we stayed in bed, narrating the sun and the grass as each strove toward the other.

*

Draw a card & draw me out: Two of Swords, reversed. I wove this blindfold while you slept and wore it beneath my eyelids. You were never one to mourn, but *to each soul its hour.*

*

We're driving the Bay Bridge. The story advances to the present, this segment of highway. *Make something up*, I say, *I'm not ready*. But it's not you, it's the radio, the script recorded long ago. Sky pours into bay, and the foundation froths. It's here!—the earthquake they warned us about. We crumple into the concrete.

*

>Moon, topaz: an effervescent pill
>fizzes and dissolves into the starless lake

ACCOMPLICE
After Octavio Paz

If you are the locked room
               I am the key that nicks the throat

If you are the trample-burr
               I am the seeking tooth

If you are the sea's leviathan blue
               I am the measure of salt

If you are the echo of rain
               I am the darkening walk

If you are the column of dust
               I am the stilted sun

If you are the heliotrope
               I am the crooked axis

If you are the midnight
               I am the slash of sleep

If you are the nearing voice
               I am the throat's seductive creak

ARS POETICA

The worm that lives inside
the landscape of my eye
elegantly writhes

a solo unrehearsed
atop the psychic scurf:
parcel of deeded earth

under no flag or anthem.
Dancing absent phantom
limbs, he cannot fathom

the loss of an essential
appendage—that elemental
disinheritance and fall

into fragment from heathen
grace. He is spared from feeling
desire newly teething.

WHY THE FILIPINO'S NOSE IS FLAT
After a Philippine myth (Nueva Ecija)

When the Galleon of Noses docked,
the race began. The Spaniards, taller
and with longer legs, hoarded the finest
features at the mass's pinnacle—

                        Dignity. Nostril
upturned, the better to smell heaven with.
Philtrum the passage to the word of God.

And for the Filipinos, the ass-end of the pile.
Peeled from the corners of crates and plunked
onto the face's fertile terrain. Misshapen.
Crushed. Vestige of the primitive.

The vessel was steered by the Editor, his
visage pearlescent against the clear of clouds.
Cartographer. Stonecarver. His Stamp of Dis-

approval seared into the underside
of every Filipino's tongue.

Minsan dowa so totol
Na tomo so parikesa.

PLANE POEM

Fibers of my mind
unspool, variegated
invisible, swooned
by mechanical wind.
The collective taste
of salt in our silence.
You are where I am not.
The edges and their coroners
loosed like beasts upon us.
What remains? A woman
thanking me for my trash.

GHOSTING MONOLOGUE

Consider me specter: no longer next to you, the sheet we lay upon drapes over me now.

My last words to you are letters in a cloud, lingering like scraps of scent. You reason: It's unreasonable to expect a response so soon. Hours pass, cling in their passing and are smelted into a day.

Days. You text again. Nothing. You think: After two more days, the last. An abundance of nothing. Briefly you convince yourself some tragedy has occurred. A vehicular mishap; the sudden expiration of a relative or dear friend. Then it becomes obvious.

The manhunt for your defects begins. In the mirror you inspect each inch of the self that stares back. Ravenous, you swallow a camera and examine your interior. Interrogate every ventricle. Blood beyond the blush. Imagine me, what is left of me that you can remember or recreate, out, with another, reveling in beauty and forgetting. Not in front of a glass, defacing the self that stares back.

My gift to you: an outline of myself, sloughing into blur. Image fades in a survey of tender dissolution. Where my face once was, a silhouette in grey. Avenues of communication closed off one by one: each concatenation clipped away.

Which question do you want least answered? *Why me?* or *Why not?*

You wish you were an hour with another hour to cling to. You despise yourself for these thoughts.

If never were I real, what of
what you said, what we did?
Does the air still hold it all?
Or have I carried it to the
afterlife—the life after you?

If I am real, I will respond. If
I am unreal—a ghost—then
you can't make me.

Make me a ghost.

Closing time. Hope empties
out your glass.

TALE OF TWO

He broke his right leg she broke her left.
O leg! Bereft. Bereft.

They twined into a ribboned knot.
Leg, sweet leg, we miss you not.

    *

Grasping
at me you grasp
also yourself.

Pain twin: desire
vibrates across our central nerve.

The dark smooths the seams.

EVERYDAY EXORCISM

For you, love
amounted to no
more than a reflecting
pool. The first poem
I read by you: the point of
view of a woman
of you.

*

Do I mourn the loss of my personal Janus? In two hours, your
two faces: from *your fault if I jump* to your anointed seat at the
head of the table, charming our friends, annihilating me.

*

You wanted me
small and silent
as your reflection's
smirk.

*

Each day more
seeps out of my pores.
Almost all my cells since then
have done the work
of annihilation.
May I turn to flame or salt
before I turn to you.

POSTSCRIPT

My dream the night of your wedding came true: I never saw you again.

MURDER CABIN

I.   Opening Credits

From within
the dark, the unmistakeable
clamor of a woman in terror.
Arbiters of disaster imprint
their names on the canvassed black.

Cut to the face and its obscurity
of mascara. Nondescript beauty
made more radiant.
High heels puncture the carpet
of leaves. She stumbles—loses one,
ditches both—staggers a barefoot
path through the undergrowth.

Cut to shadow within shadow.
The Hunter, gliding like a scythe.
This land is his land: *he knows*
it like the backside of a
hand that connects
with a woman's
face—Fade

on a scream. Bear trap
clamps the anonymous ankle.

II.   Road Trip

Youth gleams technicolor, spurning horizon.
Trunk stocked with bourbon and boxed wine.

Two women, three men. Draw
a pentagram among them: bodies

entangled or imagined entangled
in an immaterial nexus of desire. An interlude to

millennial disillusion which will transpire
in a family cabin

for the weekend, far
from the city and its bland calamities.

Everyone needs,
sometimes, to get
away.

III.   The Cabin Is

The Cabin is made of four walls, each fixed
on containment: from without, the ceaseless
fists of the elements; within, the ones who wanted
to escape—who consigned to hiatus
their habits and their brutal dullness, dreaming
that desire is endemic, that the body can
abandon it. The Cabin is surrounded
by the material of its making: scatters of
pine, still erect, plunged into soil
like syringes; injection's shadow trails
the forest floor. The Cabin is a plot on the map.
The map is inscribed on your back.

IV.   She Contemplates the Living Room Portrait

How different, even, was it, from the shrine of boy
bands plastered above the headboard of her bed: icons
clipped from magazines and collaged into guardians
of her adolescent rest, downwardly benevolent
with unadulterated smiles: blindingly pearly
screens for her girly fantasies: sweat
implied by the sheen on the arms she imagined
around her—herself become the centerfold's center,
starlet in a yellowed field of clover, her eyes meeting
in the idol's eyes her own—that altar of appetite
she lay prostrate before each night: how different
was it from the living room portrait of the life-sized
former owners: the eye first attracted to the
man in single-breasted vest austere as a contracting
star, resting his hand on the shoulder of his seated
wife's pouter pigeon blouse tapering into
the baby's christening gown: a cocoon for
a newly bewildered child of undetermined
gender, whose stare seems to pierce through
the generations into the conversation *as if
listening?* She absolves herself of the impossible
thought and follows the others to the other room.
That pageantry of virility seen off by the infant's
eyes that blink into black and morph into those
of the Hunter: hidden in a cavity between the
Cabin walls, he collapses into his infant self
and inhabits the body in which he still resides,
though here in the portrait, his father alive, and
the hands of his mother still larger than his own.

POEM

      a man at the wheel peels

            a clementine and I

wonder why

        night's funnel mouth

        spits us into memory

                  backward

DINNER PARTY

We wear all our eyes tonight: how like sequins they wink and glint.

We trade our leporine smiles and then trade them back.

In this room there is order. Cuts of meat become larger.

Silverware sentinels from the outside in.

We speak of the city's bridled gestures or the animal silence of the countryside.

Not the station of the body that cordially carries on.

Each thing knows and is in its place.

The fork, its sibylline scrape.

A delicacy of discourse: baubles spill out of our open mouths.

Consuming, consumed, we camber each to our rented rooms.

Finally—canines sharpen, grindstone-ground from desire.

A profusion of fur prevails over flesh.

In seclusion we submit, hirsute, to hunger and howl.

We bound along the borders of our dreams, under a human moon.

LOST ART

What ancestral curse am I
in the process of creating?

Another life, my skin roared *kin*
in chevron and the closed circuit

                              of a centipede
                              forming bracelet

around my bicep. This life, nothing
so permanent. I fill my well: invisible ink

extracted with an offshore drill.
I make palimpsests of mandibles.

HIBISCUS DEPTHS

My grandmother's dress washes up on the shore. Which shore? Not sure. I never saw her near water while she and I were at the same time alive. Yet coast wanes cleanly into sea, and gulls barrel through clouds, bellowing from the gutters of their throats. And there, the floral garment sashays in on a wave. Water stains the flowers darker: hibiscuses on fuchsia deepen from white to grey. The dress docks on the shoreline, vessel holding only itself.

These footprints in the sand—are they mine? I forgot where I'm going, forgot where I've been. I always suspected I was born with the wrong feet. That or the right feet screwed into the wrong ankles, their gaits bearing them perennially apart.

I call you *mother* in my mother's mother tongue. I call you into me and you come in archipelago echo.

I wear your dress. Hibiscus seeps in and patterns my skin with petals. The petals fall off. Wind's hands ferry them away, leaving me a shiver of stigma and stamen. I wear your dress. It dangles off your shoulder blades. Your ankles, your angles. I wear your dress. I put on your wrists and they soundlessly twist. I wear your dress. I wear your fists.

FABLE FOR YOUR HANDS ONLY

The messenger took my hands and turned them
Chalice / Whispered missive into the vast /
The vessel agitated with knowing / Unsound

Cargo sunk into life line / Heart line
The despot head demanded transcription
(And the neck? Bowed in genuine / genuflection)

Hands formed fists around handles
Saturated bristles in pigment / In chromatic
Stutter dyed the paper fathoms / A Rorschach

Imposter / Epistle irretrievable from the palm
(And the eyes? Pearls / inlaid into the echo shell)

CIRCLING

Those were the days of circles. Your sketchbook
pages swelled with them. Your latest obsession.
Those were the nights our friends would smoke
a bowl with us and draw circles: a procession
of eyes, forging a jagged line of sight.
Or pearls of various size—a cache of jewels
loosed from a chain and shucked of light,
transparent and laid bare in paper pools.
Believe me when I say, "Believe
you me: I circled them, those days, so long
they drained like syrup through a sieve.
Sometimes, I even know that I was wrong.
I'll give you a call. I'll tell you someday."
"I'll see it when I believe it," you'd say.

BARBIE'S DREAM HOME INVASION

I check the locks: chainlink slid into position; deadbolt bolted; the shackle on my perfect ankle still rattling. Plastic turkey forever ready in the oven, waiting to be admired. But as I yearn my mitted hand toward it, I am compelled to turn again. The door—ajar! My work, undone. Wind hisses and snakes an invisible hand under my apron. I chain, bolt, shackle again. Smooth my blonde locks. I nearly settle into my seat and then—the window! It gapes fully open; inside dissolves into outside and the essence of my signature scent, sugar cookies and gasoline, gets sucked into the night, beckoning a horde of hooligans. Though I am famed for my figure and composure, both crumble as I sink into the tile, my smile distended into silent sobs. Only from the floor can I see that my house is missing a wall. It was not damaged, but incomplete by design. The table for two, the hot pink vanity, the gauzy canopy veiling my sleep—all of it, belonging to everyone but me. Shackle, bolt, chain.

OBJECTS IN THE MIRROR ARE CLOSER THAN THEY APPEAR

Convexity of meaning: objects are larger than
they are in mirror, the mirror reducing
them to perceived insignificance as

in Western culture *bigger—thus better*;
the contrapositive holds: it assumes
not better is not bigger, or further,

objects that are not larger than they
appear are not objects in mirror—thus
to reduce an object, place it in the rear

view mirror; to increase its perceived
size, take it away—

                            the trees they

sway, and I glimpse

a fractioned decimal of this dance
circumscribed in the rearview; I look
to make myself appear larger and you

smaller, so small that you are not
in my vision at all. "Even a bear
comes down from the mountain

when it is hungry," I remember,
and in the mirror, perceive
a darkened pinprick of a bear

surfacing at mountain snow.
The trees they sway bereft
of leaves, their movements

distant shifts of bark.
With winter day comes winter dark.
Our car upon the highway arcs,

along the route we plotted on
the map. A measure of control.
We appear closer, larger.

THE WINDOW AND THE MIRROR

One prizes clarity. The other, obscurity.
One casts you

in shadow, the other aside. One mans

the periphery,
outside

only a hair-

trigger away. One
cordons vision into

amplified figure on a cinema

screen *(unseen: the hand
of a projectionist feeding*

frames into the revolving

*mechanical maw yawning
OPEN—)*. One shows

you you are one. The other: alone.

MUKBANG DIPTYCH

Noodles glut the baking tray and the video's frame: a meal meant for a large
family heaped high and red as a grade-school volcano. Beyond it are two women.

In the background: coupons secured to the fridge; obeisant row of herbs in plastic
planters. "We got ten packs here, and I am ready to die," one says as she

fills her bowl, and the other does too. *The Young-Girl is both production and a factor*
of production, that is, she is the consumer, the producer, the consumer of producers,

and the producer of consumers. "I took it to the next level like nobody would,"
says another as she coats a cob of corn with butter, mayo, and fine crimson

of powdered Cheeto. To reduce them to dust, she instructs, "Smash the Cheetos
until they're like this: pulverized." She holds her creation to the camera's eyes,

asks if we want the first bite. *The Young-Girl doesn't kiss you, she drools*
over you through her teeth. Materialism of secretions. An ethos of excess:

not "very," but "too." Quantity is worthless unless it disdains its container.
Without waiting for an answer, she wears the cob ragged with haphazard bites.

Not the balance of a ballerina, but of an accountant. Let them eat Cheetos! she does not say. Guillotine the bottom line!

The smile has never served as an argument. There is also the smile of skulls.

O RUBBER GLOVE

what forms have you known before
fleeing across the interstate?
tumbleweed-freed
from decision?

into what coerced shapes
have they seduced you
under the sun's gravel-scrape?

what corrosive sweetness
have you witnessed
withholding
judgment lacking
a mouth?

PALINODE

After "Still Life with Monkey, Fruits, and Flowers" by Jean-Baptiste Oudry

1.

Silver trough gluts with fruit:
cobalt orbs, clusters of pearls, a pyramid
of peach spheres. How indulgent,
this abandonment…—a slice of melon
ripens on the floor. Atop chipped stone,
a porphyry vase, holding flowers
in halted wilt.

2.

No the fruits had no unnatural luster
No they did not gemlike draw me
No nature was not aped
No my tail did not coil in serpentine whorls

MELANCHOLIA

As a snail
to a razor clings

flesh wound around
the edge

    *

The Fingers of God
for a moment illumine
your own

through the window caught
in your palm
blood blazing orange

*There's so much
goop inside of us and it
wants to get out*

    *

Swimming
face-first in dirt

They ask why
you don't stand
but you can't
hear them ear
pressed to soil

anguilliform
mud creature

       *

A stranger writes rent
checks with your slanted hand

gently drags you to
the shower to the next
day to the next to the
shower again

the trail
glinting with slime

X

Find the point of entry. May as well begin with molten rocks in the lagoon of space. How they hurtled toward collision the way an ambulance carves the quickest route to disaster.

Though I know better: Every story is engendered by a mother.

At a bar after, blanketed in the gauze of mute light. Numbed fingertips gripped glass. Anonymity does a body.

It does a body. It does a body into anonymity.

The constituents of a whole being inclusive of emptiness. Of what was evacuated.

What could not be evacuated.

What I think about when I cannot avoid thinking about it.

Emptiness in bed illumined by shadow. In the grocery line, cradling a pack of bitter ale. In the car, trying to drown it with sound and hot air. In the car, trying to drown.

All histories can be traced to collisions of rocks in space, the common artery for the timeline of each living thing.

Strangers on trains I saw as clumps of cells, stubbornly growing.

Children I could not bear.

All can be explained by math. Each of us a variable in a fixed equation.

Solve for x, the newfound absence.

It had been with me for weeks. Though I did not know it, I had never been alone.

Looking in the mirror made me imagine. Below the buttons, beneath the skin. Curled and floating, asleep. My benign meteor.

The photo remains in an unopened envelope with my name. The camera delved inches into me and saw.

What I close my eyes to, it saw, and it did not look away.

The phrase "point of entry" implying exit.

Perhaps our lives are set on train tracks, decisions delusions of decisions. Though some things we create. Chromosomes collide.

Pregnancy a process without mystery. Newcomer boarding a train.

At the clinic I chose the strongest medication, its effect described as similar to two or three margaritas. Struggled to keep the syringe straight while my stomach emptied itself. Still, a weight.

Still, now, a weight.

Fentanyl the drug that took me. On my back on the table I with the ceiling light buzzed.

Deep breaths, said the nurse. I *deep breath*ed to the point of bursting. Thought maybe we wouldn't make it out alive.

The vacuum sang.

The birth of Earth is imitated by that of people. Collision and growth.

Neither a mystery.

SPIRIT CANOE

The only vessel that can hold you
has no bottom. The boatswain calls
to weigh the anchor of dust and air
and you rise, grasping gunwales
with hand and foot and gazing down.
The wave of leaves of sago palm
in lieu of a goodbye. The only vessel
that can hold you has a hole, and I
fell through. I watched you go
in the spirit canoe.

BARDO AGAIN

After death, you condescend to meet me here.

●

Dress code: self, transliterated into soul. My eye dispossessed of your likeness.

●

In every picture, you are always already leaving, pointing at the sky.

●

Two fingers upright for what is spoken; the three remaining, concealing what is not.

●

Your lapis lazuli rosary fastens me to an instant.

●

Wasn't it only a matter of time? I can't help asking.

●

No: it was only matter. Only time.

ANIMAL AT THE WATERING HOLE

At the depression's edge
every sip hewn with finality and yet you still
drink to prolong

your part as innumerable pursuit

Turn not your neck
Spurn not

our foremothers'
unearned demise
sacrificed
for your sliver of life

Mirrored creature:
face yourself

Partake

PRODIGAL DAUGHTER

Day after, I wake prying at the rind
of morning, searching
for absolution,

sprawled on my childhood bed. Twin.
My father waits
in the kitchen with breakfast.

In my abandoned
apartment, another man
whose forgiveness I have

refused is waiting
for me to come home.
Though I know I won't.

Summer air heady
with calamansi flower.
Navel oranges

bloat and break
from the branch:
an offering to the chthonic,

or just a font of waste.
Give me the goods
that falleth to me.

The riotous life,
the husks meant for swine.
No man shall give

unto me. It is meet.

KANTIAN LOVE STORY

Sighting you the world blinks on. A flick of light, and then a trellis: history arced and arcing under a clamber of rose and vine. You prohibit *prior* yet the world plays along. Never and Always collapse in the diamond lattice, in the rose's hip. History arcs and aches with new weight. I was waiting for you, though with no *I*, no *was*. Before you, no me. Before you now, I petal and blanche as you hedge perennial. My body synthetic, glossy from the atoms' rush. Adamant and chlorophyll, leafy and Lethe: let us delight in light and bask in asking. Endure, endure, however impure.

NOTES

"Interesting Results of Professor Woodworth's Anthropological Studies": This is a found poem from a 1903 *New York Times* article.

"Manananggal": The manananggal is a mythical Philippine creature that poses as a woman by day, and by night, splits in half, such that the upper half sprouts wings and flies away, while the lower half is left behind. The manananggal preys on pregnant women and their unborn babies by reaching inside the womb with a proboscis-like tongue.

"Haibun in the Event of an Earthquake": The phrase "to each soul its hour" was borrowed from Frank Bidart.

"Why the Filipino's Nose is Flat": The last two lines are a Maranao proverb—"While a story may have two versions, the original is the truth."

"Mukbang Diptych": This poem references mukbang videos created by Stephanie Soo and Wendy's Eating Show. Italicized quotations are from *Preliminary Materials for a Theory of the Young-Girl* by Tiqqun.

"Melancholia": The italicized lines come from Denis Johnson, "Emergency."

ACKNOWLEDGMENTS

Thank you—

To my parents and brother, for always believing that this book would come to be.

To my teachers, for their wisdom and generosity: at the University of Utah, Jacqueline Osherow, Paisley Rekdal, and Katharine Coles; at Boston University, Karl Kirchwey, Robert Pinsky, and Maggie Dietz; and at Northwestern University, Averill Curdy and Mary Kinzie.

To my colleagues and friends in workshops over the years, for their insights and camaraderie. Special gratitude to Liza Flum, Amy Sailer, Samyak Shertok, and Kylie Millward.

To the following institutions, for their professional support: Jack Kerouac School of Disembodied Poetics, New York State Summer Writers Institute, Taft-Nicholson Center, and Vermont Studio Center.

To the editors of the following publications, in which some of these poems first appeared: *Hawai'i Review*, *hex literary*, *The Massachusetts Review*, *Nimrod International Journal*, *Salt Hill Journal*, *Strange Horizons*, and *Volume Poetry*.

To Dynamo Verlag, for taking a chance on my work.

To Derek, for everything. Each day with you in our healing home is a gift.

DYNAMO VERLAG BOOKS

Telescopes and Other People
JOSH NORMAN

Daughters of Monsters
MELISSA GOODRICH

Peregrine Nation
LUCIAN MATTISON

The Much Love Sad Dawg Trio
MATTHEW SADLER

Driving Around, Looking in Other People's Windows
CL BLEDSOE

Star Things
JESS L PARKER

On Ruben Slikk
CALEB TRUE

Local Weather
ANDREW SQUITIRO

A Human Moon
ALLELIAH NUGUID

DYNAMOVERLAG.COM

www.ingramcontent.com/pod-product-compliance
Lightning Source LLC
Chambersburg PA
CBHW030454010526
44118CB00011B/935